COUNTRY PROFILES

SOUTH SUDAN

BY AMY RECHNER

BELLWETHER MEDIA • MINNEAPOLIS, MN

Blastoff! Discovery launches
a new mission: reading to learn.
Filled with facts and features, each
book offers you an exciting new
world to explore!

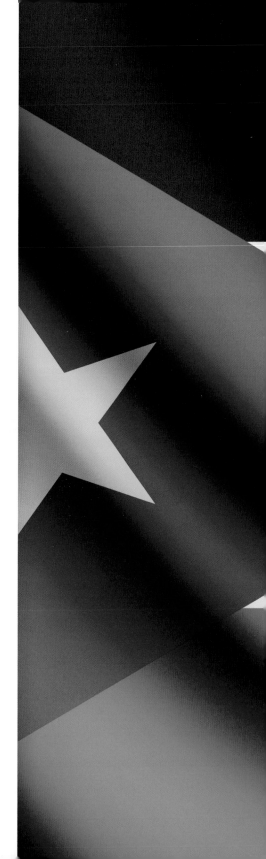

This edition first published in 2019 by Bellwether Media, Inc.

No part of this publication may be reproduced in whole or in part
without written permission of the publisher.
For information regarding permission, write to Bellwether Media, Inc.,
Attention: Permissions Department,
6012 Blue Circle Drive, Minnetonka, MN 55343.

Library of Congress Cataloging-in-Publication Data

Names: Rechner, Amy, author.
Title: South Sudan / by Amy Rechner.
Description: Minneapolis, MN : Bellwether Media, Inc., 2019. |
    Series: Blastoff! Discovery: Country Profiles | Includes
    bibliographical references and index.
Identifiers: LCCN 2018039200 (print) | LCCN 2018039676
    (ebook) | ISBN 9781681036816 (ebook) | ISBN
    9781626179639 (hardcover : alk. paper)
Subjects: LCSH: South Sudan–Juvenile literature.
Classification: LCC DT159.92 (ebook) | LCC DT159.92 .R43 2019
    (print) | DDC 962.9–dc23
LC record available at https://lccn.loc.gov/2018039200

Editor: Rebecca Sabelko   Designer: Brittany McIntosh

Printed in the United States of America, North Mankato, MN.

TABLE OF CONTENTS

Near a swampy river, a Dinka family wakes up with the January sun. Hundreds of white, long-horned cattle begin to stir. The family rubs ash from the night's fires onto their skin to protect against mosquitoes. The women milk the cows before the men take the herds to **graze**. Children collect cattle **dung** for fire fuel.

OTHER TOP SITES

BOMA NATIONAL PARK

CATHEDRAL OF ST. MARY

MOUNT KINYETI

WHITE NILE

ARM CURLS

Dinka herders cut their cattle's horns into shapes to tell the herds apart. The herders copy the shape of the horns with their arms as they move among the cattle. This shows which cattle belong to them.

The herds return to camp in the late afternoon. The tribe relaxes with music and storytelling after eating a meal. Fire smoke keeps mosquitoes away as children curl up among the cattle to sleep. This is South Sudan!

South Sudan is a **landlocked** nation located in east central Africa. The country lies just north of the **equator**. It was once part of Sudan, which lies to the north. Ethiopia is South Sudan's neighbor to the east. Kenya, Uganda, and the Democratic Republic of the Congo line the southern border. The Central African Republic sits to the west.

At 248,777 square miles (644,329 square kilometers), South Sudan is slightly smaller than Texas. The capital city of Juba sits on the Nile River in the southern part of the country.

CENTRAL AFRICAN REPUBLIC

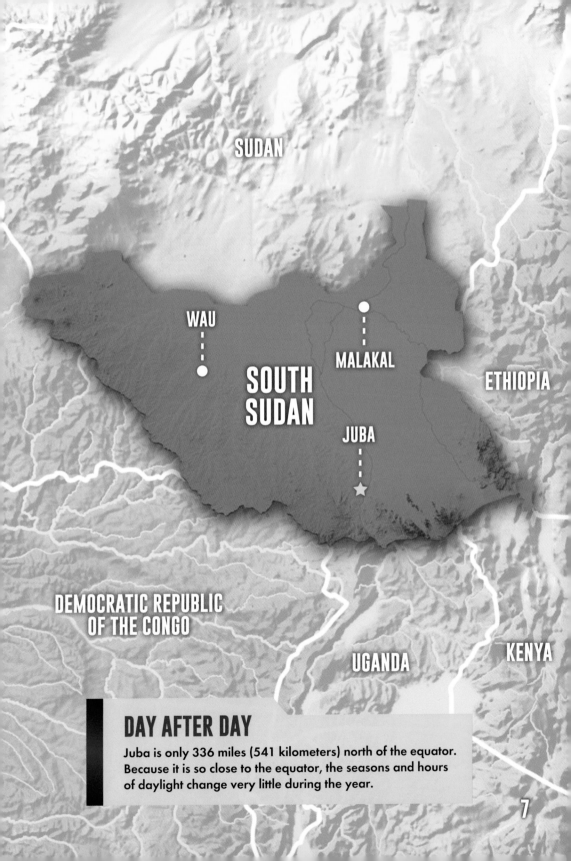

SUDAN

WAU

SOUTH
SUDAN

MALAKAL

JUBA

ETHIOPIA

DEMOCRATIC REPUBLIC
OF THE CONGO

UGANDA

KENYA

DAY AFTER DAY

Juba is only 336 miles (541 kilometers) north of the equator.
Because it is so close to the equator, the seasons and hours
of daylight change very little during the year.

LANDSCAPE AND CLIMATE

Much of South Sudan is covered in vast **plains**. The northern **savanna** is mostly grassland with some scattered trees. The White Nile snakes northward through the central Sudd, one of the largest wetlands in the world! The south is covered with woodlands. Along the Uganda border, **tropical** forests cover the Imatong Mountains.

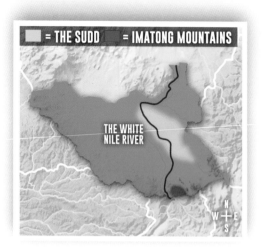

= THE SUDD   = IMATONG MOUNTAINS

THE WHITE NILE RIVER

N
W + E
S

THE SUDD

TRUE COLORS

The Nile River in South Sudan is called the White Nile. It gets the name from the light-colored clay that clouds the water. Downstream, it meets the Blue Nile.

JUBA

Average seasonal highs and lows

JANUARY
HIGH: 104 °F (40 °C)
LOW: 69 °F (21 °C)

APRIL
HIGH: 101 °F (38 °C)
LOW: 77 °F (25 °C)

JULY
HIGH: 95 °F (35 °C)
LOW: 70 °F (21 °C)

OCTOBER
HIGH: 96 °F (36 °C)
LOW: 73 °F (23 °C)

°F = degrees Fahrenheit
°C = degrees Celsius

NILE RIVER

South Sudan has a tropical climate with two seasons. The wet season lasts from April to November. The weather is hot, rainy, and humid. The dry winter season brings cooler air and little rain.

WILDLIFE

The savannas of South Sudan welcome many types of wildlife. The Sudd and surrounding plains are home to antelope like white-eared kobs and topis that form **migrating** herds in the millions. Boma National Park in the east attracts animals from all over Africa. Zebras and ostriches race to safety while lions hunt for prey. Elephants guard their young among the trees.

Crocodiles creep along the Nile. Mosquitoes buzz in swamps, and tsetse flies swarm in woodlands. The **rain forests** shelter baboons, chimpanzees, and giant pangolins. Leopards live in the trees, while African golden cats stalk below. Cranes and hippopotamuses splash in the rivers.

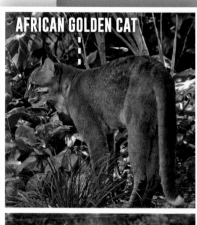
AFRICAN GOLDEN CAT

OSTRICH

GIANT PANGOLIN

ZEBRAS

ELEPHANTS

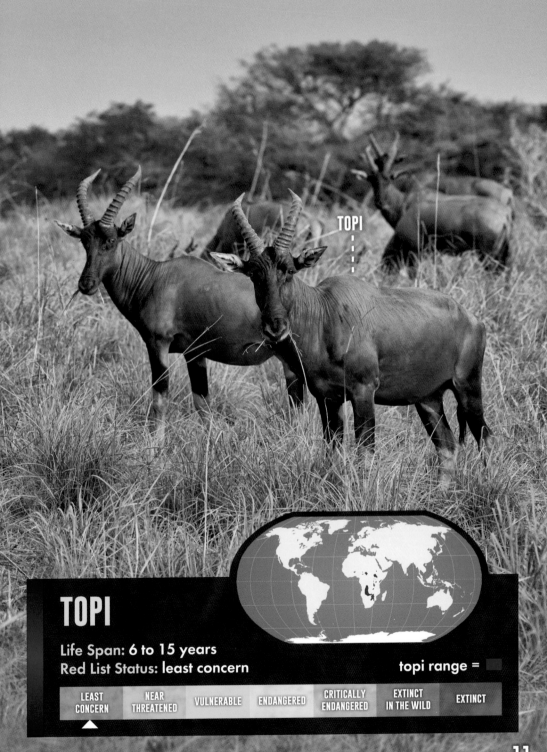

TOPI

TOPI

Life Span: 6 to 15 years
Red List Status: least concern

topi range =

| LEAST CONCERN | NEAR THREATENED | VULNERABLE | ENDANGERED | CRITICALLY ENDANGERED | EXTINCT IN THE WILD | EXTINCT |

Most of the 13 million South Sudanese are Africans from different **ethnic** groups. The largest group is the Dinka. They are cattle herders, as are the Nuer. These two groups have been in a harmful **civil war** for many years. Other groups like the Shilluk live on farms in settlements.

South Sudan broke from Sudan to escape strict Islamic laws, although a small **Arab** population remains. Many people speak Arabic, but the official language is now English. More than half the population is Christian. Each ethnic group also has its own language and faith. Many still practice their **traditions**. They often combine them with Christian **rituals**.

FAMOUS FACE

Name: **Alek Wek**
Birthday: **April 16, 1977**
Hometown: **Wau, South Sudan**
Famous for: **A supermodel who fled from war-torn South Sudan at age 14, Wek is an ambassador to the United Nations Refugee Agency and works to help people in need around the world**

SPEAK ARABIC

Arabic uses script instead of letters. However, Arabic words can be written with the English alphabet so you can read them.

ENGLISH	ARABIC	HOW TO SAY IT
hello	marhaban	mar-HAB-ah
goodbye	ma'a as-salama	ma ahs-sah-LAH-mah
please (to males)	min fadlak	min FAHD-lehck
please (to females)	min fadlik	min FAHD-lick
thank you	shukran	SHUH-krahn
yes	na'am	NAHM
no	laa	LAH-ah

Most South Sudanese live in **rural** villages or on farms. Many live near rivers or lakes for access to water. A typical home is a tall, circular mud brick hut called a *tukul*. Rural families group their *tukuls* together. **Nomads** travel with livestock in search of grass, carrying their belongings.

LOW ENERGY

Rural areas do not have electricity. Only 1 in 25 city dwellers do, but the power is limited. Most of South Sudan's people live without it.

TUKUL HUTS

Only one in five people live in a city. They have apartments or small houses. Some use traditional furniture like grass mats and benches. Others use European furniture like sofas and beds. South Sudan has few paved roads. The Nile serves as an important way to move through the country.

South Sudanese value their tribe above anything else. Most tribes share traditions through storytelling, songs, and rituals. Some use body art to celebrate special life moments. Marriages are carefully planned because the two families will be strongly connected. Couples have many children who carry on the tribal customs and keep the community strong.

Most people wear Western-style clothing. Some women wear the *tobe*, a bright fabric that is loosely wrapped around the body. They wear a lot of jewelry. Most of it is made from handmade beads. Bead decoration is found on men's clothing, too.

HANDMADE BEADS

IMPORTANT NAMES

Dinka and Nuer children are named after the colors of their cattle. Supermodel Alek Wek is from the Dinka tribe. Her name means "black-and-white cow."

WORD WALL

When South Sudan won its independence in 2011, the new president declared English as the country's new official language. Although there are few English-speaking teachers, schools must now teach in English.

Decades of civil war between the Dinka and Nuer have made schooling difficult. One in four people knows how to read. Many students must leave school to work or move to safety. The country lacks teachers and resources. But it offers eight years of primary school to children with limited access to education.

Most South Sudanese raise crops and livestock. They are **subsistence farmers** who eat what they grow. **Commercial** farms grow peanuts and sugar cane for **export**. Factory workers make many food products. People in the cities have **service jobs** in shops, restaurants, or government offices.

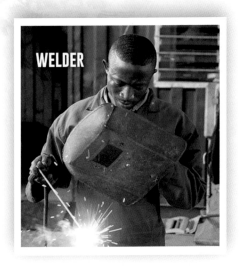

WELDER

FARMERS

SOCCER

Soccer is the top sport in South Sudan. Some kids make their own soccer balls to play with. Basketball and volleyball are also popular. Wrestling matches often attract crowds who cheer as young men from different ethnic groups wrestle. Singing, dancing, and drumming add to the excitement.

WRESTLING

South Sudanese **culture** is full of music. Many ethnic groups use music in their storytelling. City cafes host concerts. Many people enjoy card games and talking to pass the time.

MUSIC

MAKE YOUR OWN BEADS

What You Need:
- mixing bowl
- 4 cups flour
- 1 cup salt
- food coloring
- baking tray
- toothpick
- paint or permanent markers

Instructions:
1. With an adult, preheat oven to 250 degrees Fahrenheit (121 degrees Celsius).
2. In the bowl, mix the flour, salt, and food coloring. Add water and stir until it becomes dough.
3. Knead the dough for about 15 minutes.
4. Pinch off a small amount of the dough. Mold the dough into any shape or size you choose.
5. Using a toothpick, make a hole through the bead. Place the bead on the baking tray. Repeat.
6. With the help of an adult, place the beads in the oven, and bake for about 2-3 minutes. They are ready when they are dry and firm.
7. Allow the beads to cool before you decorate them with paint or permanent markers. They are ready to use when they are dry!

21

FILL ME UP

Asīda is so thick that it is used as a spoon. People pinch off a chunk of asīda, mold it into a spoon shape, and use it to scoop food into their mouths.

Across South Sudan, grains like millet and sorghum are food **staples**. Okra, peanuts, and beans are also important. Shilluk farmers often raise goats, sheep, and cattle. Nomadic tribes like the Nuer and Dinka drink cow's milk and eat fish from nearby rivers.

Most South Sudanese eat their first meal around midday. It might be milky tea and *kisra*, a flatbread, or *walwal*, a thin sorghum porridge served with vegetables and a peanut butter sauce or spices. A late dinner of fish, meat, or okra stew known as *bamya* is eaten with *asīda*, a thick sorghum porridge.

OKRA

SORGHUM

SOUTH SUDANESE TOMATO SALAD

Ingredients:
3 fresh tomatoes
2 green onions
1/2 cup fresh parsley

Dressing:
1/3 cup vegetable or light olive oil
1/4 cup unsweetened, creamy peanut butter
2 limes, juiced
1/4 teaspoon cayenne pepper

Steps:
1. Wash the tomatoes. With the help of an adult, chop the tomatoes into small pieces. Put them in a large bowl.

2. Rinse the green onions. Peel the outside layer of skin off the bulbs. Slice the greens to the tops of the bulbs.

3. Wash and dry the parsley. Pull the leaves off the stems. Measure 1/2 cup of leaves. Chop or tear them before tossing into a bowl. Mix all vegetables well.

4. In a small bowl, whisk together the oil, peanut butter, lime juice, and cayenne pepper. Give it a taste, and adjust seasonings as desired.

5. Refrigerate bowls separately until it is time to serve the salad. Then pour the dressing over the tomato mixture, toss, and serve!

The springtime *Hagana* Festival celebrates peace, harmony, and the arts. Performers from all over the country bring music, theater, and dance to Juba. South Sudan's Independence Day is July 9. This new country is still deciding how to honor its fight for freedom. Many visit John Garang Memorial Park in Juba.

The most celebrated holiday is Christmas. The outside walls of houses are painted with detailed patterns. Everyone wears their finest clothes to church. They come home to a feast and music with family and friends. The South Sudanese people cherish their traditions and families above all!

HAGANA

INDEPENDENCE
DAY

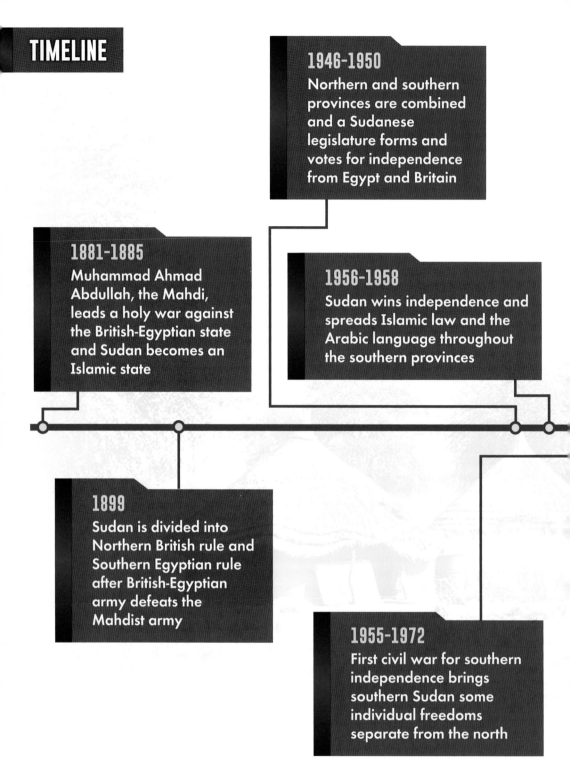

1946-1950
Northern and southern provinces are combined and a Sudanese legislature forms and votes for independence from Egypt and Britain

1881-1885
Muhammad Ahmad Abdullah, the Mahdi, leads a holy war against the British-Egyptian state and Sudan becomes an Islamic state

1956-1958
Sudan wins independence and spreads Islamic law and the Arabic language throughout the southern provinces

1899
Sudan is divided into Northern British rule and Southern Egyptian rule after British-Egyptian army defeats the Mahdist army

1955-1972
First civil war for southern independence brings southern Sudan some individual freedoms separate from the north

2017
Government and rebels sign cease fire in hopes of rescuing peace agreement

1983-2005
Second civil war begins when freedoms are taken away and Islamic law is imposed

2011
South Sudanese vote for full independence from Sudan and citizens flee war zones and famine in Sudan and South Sudan

2013
A new civil war breaks out when President Kiir, a Dinka, accused Vice President Machar, a Nuer, of plotting to overthrow the government

Official Name: Republic of South Sudan

Flag of South Sudan: Three equal horizontal bands of black, red, and green, with thin stripes of white above and below the red. A blue triangle with its base on the left side points to the center. Black stands for the people, red for bloodshed in the struggle for freedom, green for the land, and blue for the waters of the Nile. A gold star in the middle of the triangle stands for the unity of South Sudan's states.

Area: 248,777 square miles
  (644,329 square kilometers)

Capital City: Juba

Important Cities: Wau, Malakal

Population:
  13,026,129 (July 2017)

WHERE PEOPLE LIVE

COUNTRYSIDE
80.4%

CITY
19.6%

JOBS

SERVICES
13%

MANUFACTURING
7%

FARMING
80%

Main Exports:

petroleum

gum arabic

National Holiday:
Independence Day (July 9)

Main Languages:
English and Arabic

Form of Government:
presidential republic

Title for Country Leaders:
president and vice president

RELIGION

CHRISTIAN
60%

OTHER
40%

Unit of Money:
South Sudanese pound

GLOSSARY

Arab—related to people who are originally from the Arabian Peninsula

civil war—a war between groups of people in the same country

commercial—made or grown to be sold for profit

culture—the beliefs, arts, and ways of life in a place or society

dung—solid waste from an animal

equator—an imaginary circle around the Earth equally distant from the north and south poles

ethnic—related to a group of people who share customs and an identity

export—to sell to a different country

graze—to eat grass or other plants that are growing in a field or pasture

landlocked—completely surrounded by land

migrating—traveling from one place to another, often with the seasons

nomads—people with no fixed home who wander from place to place

plains—large areas of flat land

rain forests—thick, green forests that receive a lot of rain

rituals—religious ceremonies or practices

rural—related to the countryside

savanna—an African grassland containing scattered trees

service jobs—jobs that perform tasks for people or businesses

staples—widely used foods or other items

subsistence farmers—farmers who use all the crops and animals they raise

traditions—customs, ideas, or beliefs handed down from one generation to the next

tropical—related to the tropics; the tropics is a hot, rainy region near the equator.

TO LEARN MORE

AT THE LIBRARY

Koontz, Robin. *Learning About Africa*. Minneapolis, Minn.: Lerner Publications, 2016.

Rodger, Ellen. *A Refugee's Journey from South Sudan*. New York, N.Y.: Crabtree Publishing Company, 2018.

Steele, Philip. *Sudan, Darfur, and the Nomadic Conflicts*. New York, N.Y.: Rosen Pub., 2013.

ON THE WEB

FACTSURFER

Factsurfer.com gives you a safe, fun way to find more information.

1. Go to www.factsurfer.com.

2. Enter "South Sudan" into the search box.

3. Click the "Surf" button and select your book cover to see a list of related web sites.

INDEX

The images in this book are reproduced through the courtesy of: Gallo Images/ Alamy, front cover, p. 5 (top); John Wollwerth, pp. 4-5, 9 (top), 12, 13 (bottom), 14, 15, 20 (top, bottom); Frederique Cifuentes Morgan/ Alamy, p. 5 (middle top); Wikipedia, p. 5 (middle bottom); Adriana Mahdalova, p. 5 (bottom); Yann Arthus-Bertrand/ Getty Images, p. 8; John Wollwerth, p. 9 (top); Frontpage, p. 9 (bottom); Johan W. Elzenga, p. 10 (left); Graeme Knox, p. 10 (top); paula french, p. 10 (middle top); Eugene Troskie, p. 10 (middle bottom); Volodymyr Burdiak, p. 10 (bottom); Juergen Ritterbach/ Alamy, pp. 10-11; Everett Collection, p. 13 (top); vario images, Inh. Susanne Baumgarten e.K./ Alamy, p. 16; Irene Abdou/ Alamy, pp. 16-17; Sean Sprague/ Alamy, pp. 18, 21 (top); Agencja Fotograficzna Caro/ Alamy, p. 19 (top); Paul Jeffrey/ Alamy, p. 19 (bottom); Nataly Reinch, p. 21 (bottom); Joerg Boethling/ Alamy, p. 22 (right); Kelvin Wong, p. 23 (top); HelloRF Zcool, p. 23 (middle); Fanfo, p. 23 (bottom); Ragnhild Gylver/ Alamy, p. 24; Paula Bronstein/ Staff/ Getty Images, pp. 24-25; Glyn Thomas/ Alamy, p. 29 (currency).